100 facts
Explorers

100 facts Explorers

Dan North
Consultant: Fiona Macdonald

Miles Kelly

First published in 2005 by Miles Kelly Publishing Ltd
Harding's Barn, Bardfield End Green, Thaxted, Essex, CM6 3PX

This edition printed in 2014

6 8 10 9 7

Publishing Director: Belinda Gallagher
Creative Director: Jo Cowan
Editor: Rosalind Neave
Assistant Editor: Lucy Dowling
Volume Designer: Elaine Wilkinson
Picture Researchers: Jennifer Cozens, Liberty Newton
Proofreader: Margaret Berrill
Indexer: Jane Parker
Production Manager: Elizabeth Collins
Reprographics: Stephan Davis, Anthony Cambray, Liberty Newton, Ian Paulyn
Assets: Lorraine King

ISBN 978-1-84236-877-0

Printed in China

British Library Cataloguing-in-Publication Data
A catalogue record for this book is available from the British Library

ACKNOWLEDGEMENTS
The publishers would like to thank the following artists who have contributed to this book:

Peter Dennis, Mike Foster, Terry Gabbey, Richard Hook, John James, Janos Marffy, Mike Saunders, Gwen Tourret, Mike White

Cartoons by Mark Davis at Mackerel

All other artworks from the Miles Kelly Artwork Bank

The publishers would like to thank the following sources for the use of their photographs:

Page 30 (B) CORBIS; Page 41 (T) The Art Archive;
Page 42 (FP) Robert Holmes/CORBIS

All other images from the Miles Kelly Archives

Made with paper from a sustainable forest

www.mileskelly.net
info@mileskelly.net

Contents

The first explorers

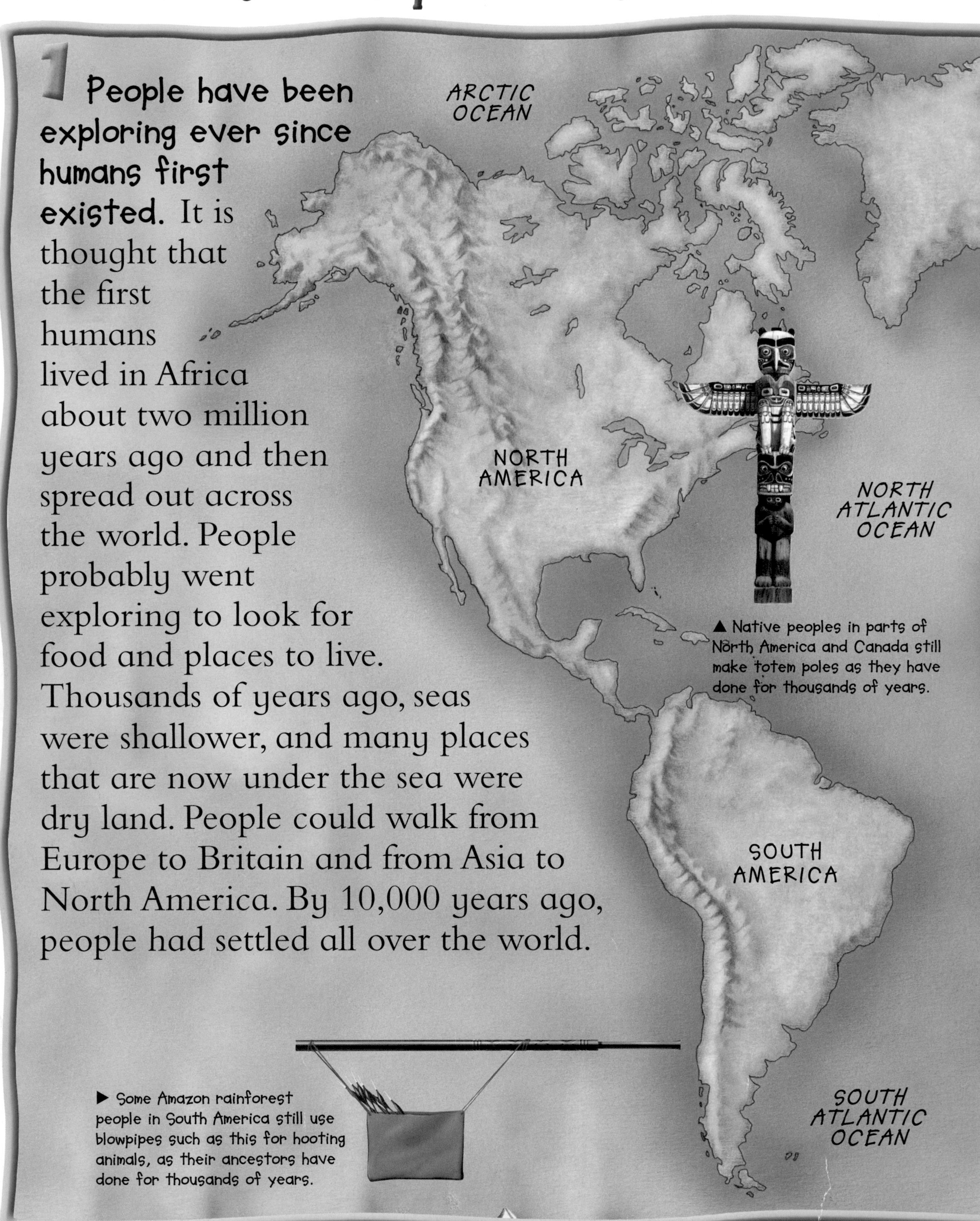

1 People have been exploring ever since humans first existed. It is thought that the first humans lived in Africa about two million years ago and then spread out across the world. People probably went exploring to look for food and places to live. Thousands of years ago, seas were shallower, and many places that are now under the sea were dry land. People could walk from Europe to Britain and from Asia to North America. By 10,000 years ago, people had settled all over the world.

▲ Native peoples in parts of North America and Canada still make totem poles as they have done for thousands of years.

▶ Some Amazon rainforest people in South America still use blowpipes such as this for hooting animals, as their ancestors have done for thousands of years.

The first explorers had to rely on their observations of the Moon and stars and on not sailing too far from land in order to find their way.

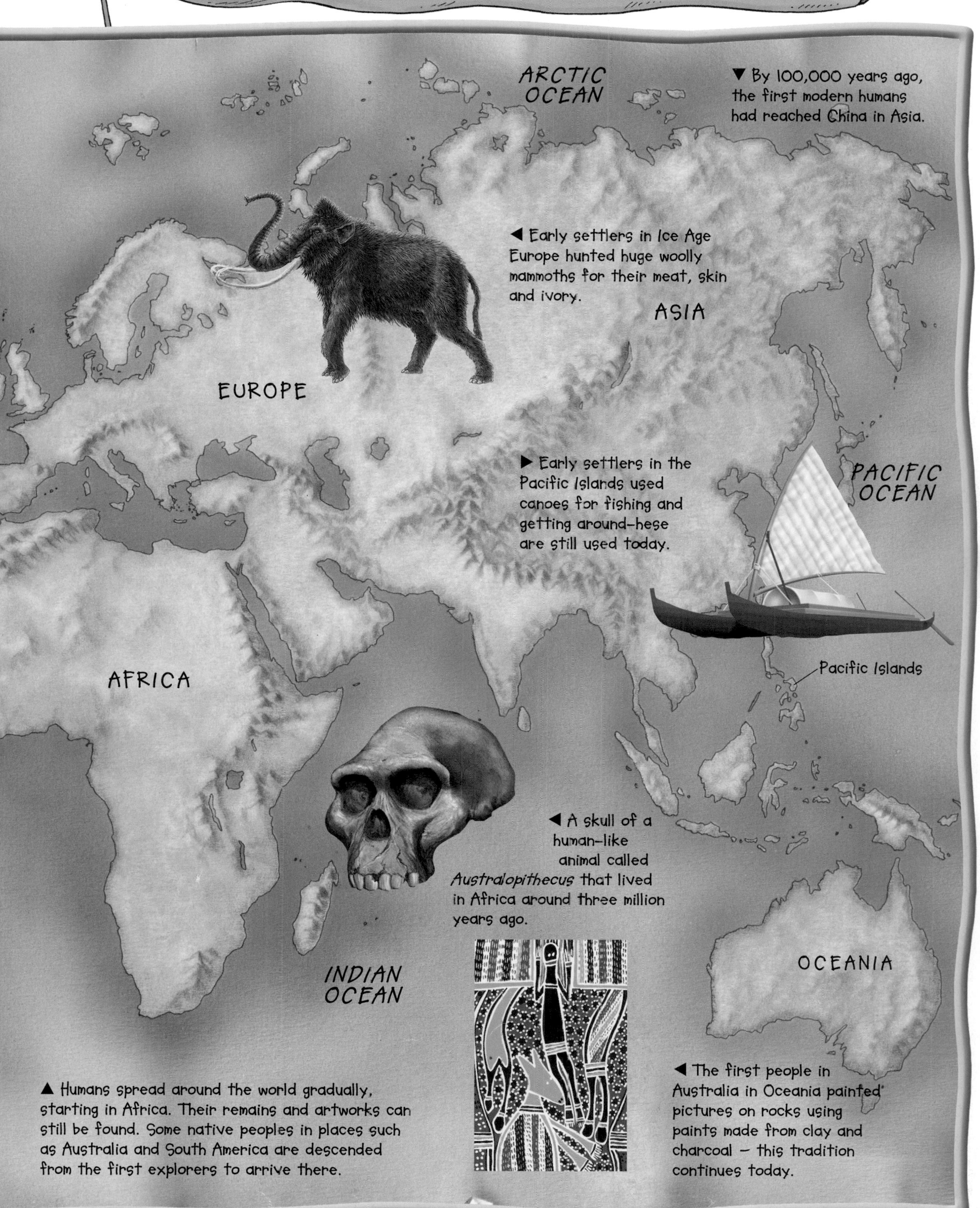

▼ By 100,000 years ago, the first modern humans had reached China in Asia.

◀ Early settlers in Ice Age Europe hunted huge woolly mammoths for their meat, skin and ivory.

▶ Early settlers in the Pacific Islands used canoes for fishing and getting around–hese are still used today.

◀ A skull of a human-like animal called *Australopithecus* that lived in Africa around three million years ago.

▲ Humans spread around the world gradually, starting in Africa. Their remains and artworks can still be found. Some native peoples in places such as Australia and South America are descended from the first explorers to arrive there.

◀ The first people in Australia in Oceania painted pictures on rocks using paints made from clay and charcoal – this tradition continues today.

Ancient adventurers

2 The ancient Greeks and Egyptians were great explorers, building boats to sail the oceans. Their kings and queens had enough money to pay for big exploring trips. They sent explorers to look for new lands, collect treasure and meet peoples from other parts of the world.

◀ An ancient Egyptian carving of Harkhuf.

3 Harkhuf of Egypt went exploring more than 4000 years ago. His king, Pharaoh Merenre, sent him to explore the land of Yam (now part of Sudan in Africa). Harkhuf brought back gifts of precious ivory, spices and wild animals such as leopards.

4 Egyptian Queen Hatshepsut sent explorers to look for a magical land she had heard about. The land, called Punt, was said to be full of treasure and beautiful animals. It was probably part of present-day Somalia, in Africa. Hatshepsut's sailors set off to find Punt. They brought back gold, ivory, monkeys, perfumes and special oils and resins, from which the Egyptians made make-up for their faces.

The ancient Egyptians thought the world was flat and rectangular, with the sea running around the edge!

▼ For long-distance journeys, the Phoenicians used ships with both sails and oars.

5 In ancient times, the best sailors of all were the Phoenicians (say 'fuh-nee-shuns'). They came from what is now Syria and Lebanon and sailed all over the Mediterranean Sea. In 600BC, an Egyptian king, Pharaoh Necho II, asked a crew of Phoenicians to see if they could sail all the way around Africa. The trip took them three years. It was 2000 years before anyone sailed around Africa again. The Phoenicians used the stars to help them navigate (find their way).

6 Pytheas was an ancient Greek who explored the icy north between 380 and 310BC. He sailed out of the Mediterranean Sea, past Spain and Britain, and discovered a cold land he named Thule. This might have been Iceland, or part of Norway. Pytheas was the first Greek to see icebergs, the northern lights, and the Sun shining at midnight. However, when he returned to Greece, few people believed his stories.

◀ Hatshepsut stayed at home attending to her duties as queen, while her sailors set off to look for Punt.

I DON'T BELIEVE IT!

When he was sailing past Scotland, Pytheas was amazed to see fish the size of boats. In fact they weren't fish at all – they were whales!

Marco Polo

7 Marco Polo is one of the most famous explorers of all time. Marco lived in Venice in Italy in the 1200s and travelled to Asia at a time when most people in Europe never ventured far from their home village. Altogether, Marco travelled over 40,000 kilometres.

◀ When Marco Polo visited Far Eastern lands such as China, hardly anyone in Europe had ever been there.

◀ This map shows Marco Polo's route across Asia. The journey home took three years.

8 Marco Polo started exploring when he was just 17 years old. His father and uncle were merchants who went to the Far East on business. When Marco was old enough, they took him with them. In 1271, they all set off for China – a journey that took them three years.

9 In China, the Polos stayed with a mighty emperor called Kublai Khan. He had enormous palaces, rooms full of treasure, and many wives and servants. Kublai Khan gave Marco the job of travelling around his lands to bring him news. Marco went all over China and Southeast Asia.

On the way to China, Marco Polo crossed the vast, empty Desert of Lop, now called the Gobi Desert.

▲ Coal, fireworks, eyeglasses, ice cream, pasta and paper money were some of the things Marco saw for the first time on his travels.

10

On his travels through Asia, Marco Polo discovered all kinds of amazing inventions. He saw fireworks, coal, paper money, pasta, ice cream and eyeglasses for the first time. He was also impressed to find that the Chinese had a postage system and could post each other letters.

11

After 20 years away, the Polos were ready to go home. They sailed most of the way in a junk – a Chinese sailing ship. More than 600 passengers and crew died of diseases on the way, but the Polos got home to Venice safely in 1295.

12

Later, there was a war in Italy and Marco Polo was captured. He ended up sharing a prison cell with a writer, and told him his life story. The writer wrote down Marco's travel tales to make a book called *The Travels of Marco Polo*. It became a bestseller!

TRUE OR FALSE?

1. In Indonesia, Marco met human beings with tails.
2. A junk is a type of carriage.
3. Christopher Columbus loved reading Marco Polo's book.
4. Marco discovered pizza in China.

Answers:
1. FALSE In his book, Marco said men with tails existed, but he never saw them himself. Now we know it was just an old wives' tale.
2. FALSE It is a type of ship.
3. TRUE Reading Marco Polo's book inspired Columbus to become an explorer.
4. FALSE He discovered pasta, not pizza.

Ibn Battuta

13 Ibn Battuta became an explorer because of a dream. Battuta was visiting Mecca, the Muslim holy city, in 1325. There he dreamed that a giant bird picked him up and carried him away. Battuta thought the dream was a message from God, telling him to go exploring. Since he was a Muslim, he decided to visit every Muslim country in the world.

14 Ibn Battuta set off on his travels, and kept going for nearly 30 years! He visited more than 40 countries, including present-day Kenya, Iran, Turkey, India and China. Just as he had planned, he visited every Muslim land that existed at the time. Altogether, he travelled more than 120,000 kilometres.

▶ India's Sultan, Muhammad Tughluq, was violent and cruel.

15 Ibn Battuta stayed in India for seven years, working for the Sultan. Battuta's job was to be a judge, deciding whether people charged with crimes were innocent or guilty. Battuta was afraid of the Sultan, who was cruel. If anyone disagreed with him, he would have them boiled, beheaded or skinned alive. Once, he nearly beheaded Battuta for being friends with a man he didn't like.

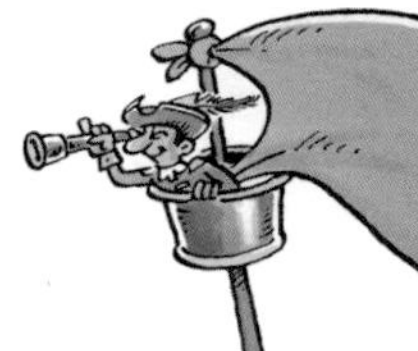

When Battuta set out to travel the world he was only 20 years old. He didn't return home until he was 47!

▼ Ibn Battuta's travels began after he dreamed of setting off to the East, carried by a giant bird.

16 **Ibn Battuta was lucky to finish his travels alive.** During his journey, Battuta was attacked by robbers in India, kept prisoner in the Maldives, chased by pirates in Sri Lanka and shipwrecked several times. At the end of his journey, he saw people suffering from the Black Death, a terrible and deadly disease. Fortunately Battuta managed to avoid catching it.

17 **At last, Ibn Battuta went home to Morocco, his own country.** When the Sultan heard about his adventures, he asked Battuta to write them all down for him. Battuta didn't have to do the writing himself, though. Instead, he told his story to a scribe (writer) who wrote it all down for him. The finished book was called the *Rihala*, meaning the travels.

I DON'T BELIEVE IT!

In many of the places he visited, Ibn Battuta got married. He had several wives and children in different parts of the world.

Chinese explorers

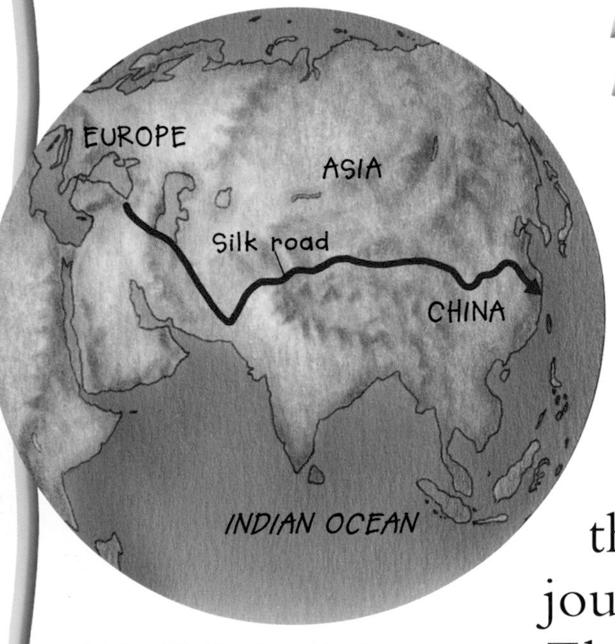

▲ The Silk Road reached across Asia, from Europe to China.

18 Some of the greatest ever explorers came from China. The first was a soldier, Zhang Qian, who lived around 114BC. The Chinese emporer sent him to find a tribe called the Yueh-Chih, who they hoped would help them fight their enemies, the Huns. On their journey, the Huns captured Zhang Qian and put him in prison for ten years.

When he finally escaped and found the Yueh-Chih, they said they didn't want to help!

19 The explorer Xuan Zang was banned from going exploring, but he went anyway. The Chinese emperor wanted him to work in a temple but Xuan Zang wanted to go to India to learn about his religion, Buddhism. In the year 629, he sneaked out of China and followed the Silk Road to Afghanistan. Then he went south to India. Xuan Zang returned 16 years later, with a collection of Buddhist holy books and statues. The emperor was so pleased, he forgave Xuan Zang and gave him a royal welcome.

MAKE A COMPASS

On his travels, Zheng He used a compass to find his way about.

You will need:

magnet water large bowl piece of wood a real compass

1. Half-fill the large bowl with water.
2. Place the wood in the water with the magnet on top, making sure they do not touch the sides.
3. When the wood is still, the magnet will be pointing to the North and South Poles. You can even check the position with a real compass.

20 **By the 1400s, the Chinese were exploring the world.** Their best explorer was a sailor named Zheng He. Zheng He used huge Chinese junks to sail right across the Indian Ocean as far as Africa. Wherever he went, Zheng He collected all kinds of precious stones, plants and animals to take back to China to show the emperor. The present that the emperor liked most was a giraffe from East Africa.

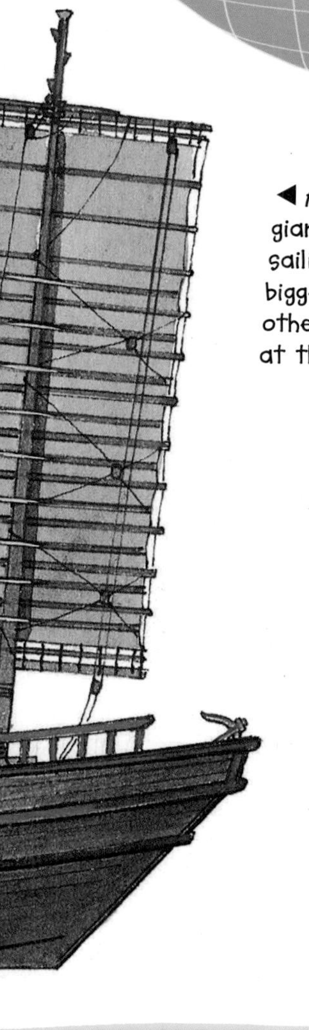

◀ A junk was a giant Chinese sailing ship, bigger than any other ships built at the time.

◀ The Chinese emperor was thrilled when Zheng He presented him with a live giraffe.

21 **Zheng He's junks were the largest sailing ships on Earth.** The biggest was 130 metres long and 60 metres wide. On a typical expedition, Zheng He would take 300 ships and over a thousand crew members, as well as doctors, map-makers, writers, blacksmiths and gardeners. The gardeners grew fruit and vegetables in pots on the decks, so that there would be plenty of food for everyone.

Sailing around Africa

▼ Spices are cheap today, but in the Middle Ages they were worth their weight in gold – at least!

Ginger

Mace

Nutmeg

22 In Europe in the 1400s, people loved spices. They used the strong-tasting seeds and leaves to flavour food and make medicines. Nutmeg, cloves, ginger and pepper came from Asian countries such as India. The spices had to be transported on camels across Asia and Europe, which took a long time. They wanted to find a way to sail from Europe to Asia, to make the journey easier.

23 The best way to sail to Asia was around Africa. But nobody knew how. A Portuguese prince named Henry (1394–1460) started a sailing school to train sailors for the task and began sending ships around the coast of Africa. At first, the sailors were too scared to sail very far because they thought the Atlantic Ocean was too stormy and dangerous. But slowly they sailed further and further.

◀ Henry the Navigator never went exploring himself. He just organized expeditions and paid sailors to go on them.

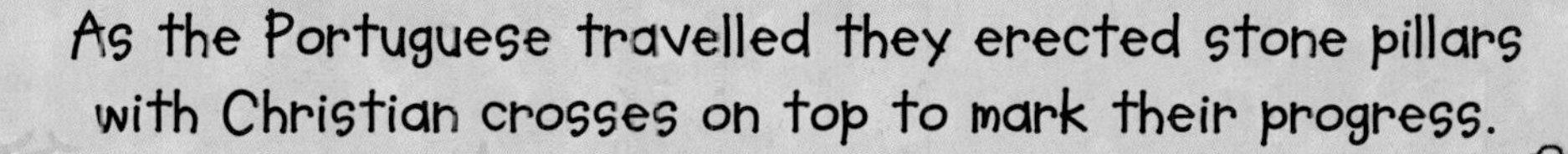

24

In 1488, a captain named Bartolomeu Dias sailed around the bottom of Africa into the Indian Ocean. Dias had a rough journey, so he named the southern tip of Africa The Cape of Storms. It was renamed The Cape of Good Hope to make sailors think it was safe.

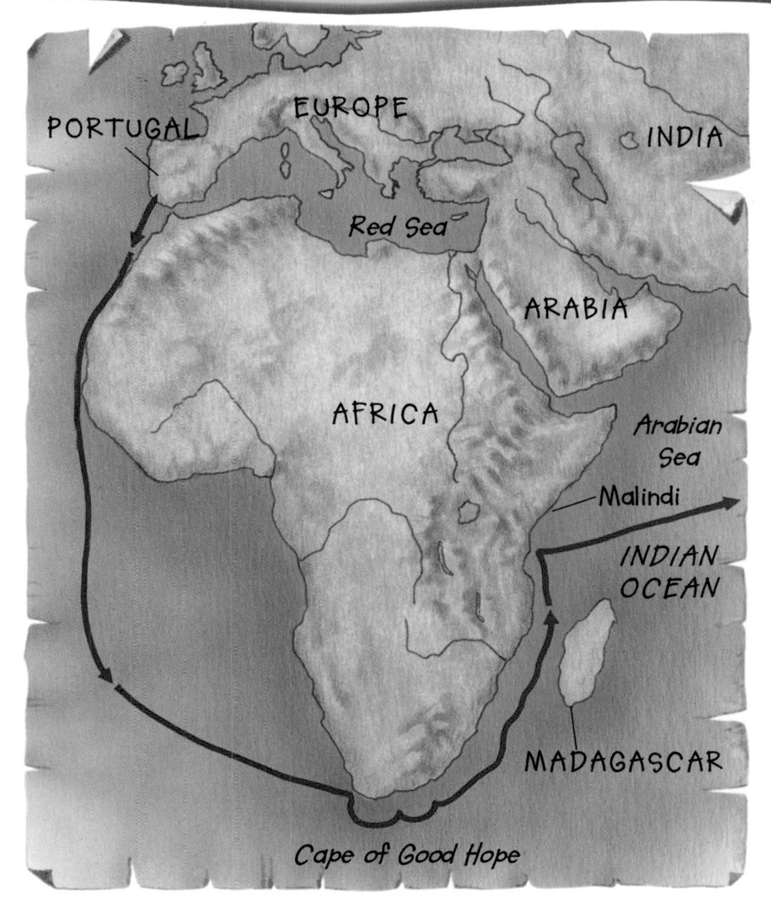

▲ Vasco da Gama sailed from Portugal, right around the southern tip of Africa and up the east coast, before crossing the Indian Ocean to India.

25

In 1497, a Portuguese sailor finally sailed around the coast of Africa. His name was Vasco da Gama. After sailing around the Cape of Good Hope, da Gama sailed up the east coast of Africa to Malindi. From there he crossed the Indian Ocean to Calicut in India. Here he hoped to buy spices, but the Rajah, Calicut's ruler, told da Gama he would have to come back with some gold. Da Gama went home empty-handed, but the king of Portugal was very happy. The sea route to Asia had been found, and many traders used it from then on.

◀ Besides being a sea captain, Vasco da Gama was a wealthy nobleman, as his grand outfit shows.

Discovering America

26 Lots of people think Christopher Columbus discovered America, but he didn't. The Vikings were the first to sail there, in around the year 1000. They found a land with lots of trees, fish and berries, and called it Vinland. They didn't stay long – they went home after getting into fights with the native Americans. After that, many people forgot that Vinland existed.

▶ The *Santa Maria* was the leader of Columbus' fleet of ships. She was about 23 metres long and had three masts and five sails.

27 Almost 500 years later, Christopher Columbus found America – by mistake! Columbus set sail from Spain in 1492, with three ships called the *Santa Maria*, the *Nina* and the *Pinta*. Columbus wasn't looking for a new land. Instead, he wanted to sail right around the Earth to find a new route to Asia, where he planned to buy spices. Although he was Italian, it was Queen Isabella of Spain who gave Columbus money for his trip.

Columbus never stopped thinking he'd found part of Asia, and died in 1506 still refusing to believe the New World existed.

28 When Columbus found land, he was sure he'd sailed to Japan. In fact, Columbus had found the Bahamas, which are close to American mainland.

29 Back in Spain, no one believed Columbus' story. They knew he couldn't have reached China in such a short time. Instead, they realized he must have found a brand new country. People called the new country the New World, and many more explorers set off at once to see it for themselves.

▲ Columbus and two of his men stepping ashore on the Bahamas, to be greeted by the local people.

30 America wasn't named after Columbus. Instead, it was named after another famous explorer, Amerigo Vespucci. In 1507, a map-maker put Amerigo's name on a map of the New World, and changed it from Amerigo to America. The name stuck.

31 It's thanks to Columbus that Native Americans were known as Indians. Since he thought he was in Asia, Columbus called the lands he found the West Indies, and the people he met Indians. They are still called this today – even though America is nowhere near India.

The Conquistadors

32 'Conquistador' is a Spanish word that means conqueror. The Conquistadors were Spanish soldiers and noblemen who lived in the 1500s. After Christopher Columbus discovered America in 1492, the Conquistadors set off to explore the new continent. Many of them wanted to get rich by grabbing all the land, gold and jewels they could find in America.

▲ The Aztecs often used the precious stone turquoise in their art. This mask is covered in tiny turquoise tiles.

◀ Leoncico, Balboa's dog, was always at his master's side as he trekked through the forest.

33 Vasco Nuñez de Balboa was one of the first Conquistadors. He sailed to America in 1500 to look for treasure. In 1513, Balboa trekked through the jungle with his dog, Leoncico, and an army of soldiers. He was the first European to cross America and see the Pacific Ocean on the other side. Balboa loved his dog so much, he paid him a wage like the soldiers. But like most Conquistadors, Balboa could be cruel too – he killed many local people and stole their gold.

People in South and Central America still speak Spanish thanks to the Conquistadors' conquests.

34 **Hernan Cortes was a very cunning Conquistador.** In 1519, he went to what is now Mexico, to conquer the Aztec people. When he arrived at their city, Tenochtitlan, the people thought he was a god. Cortes captured their king, Montezuma, and took over the city. Montezuma was killed by his own people. Then, after lots of fighting, Cortes took control of the whole Aztec empire.

EXPLORER QUIZ

1. What was Vasco Nuñez de Balboa's dog called?
2. What did the Aztecs do to make their gods happy?
3. What did the Inca king offer Pizarro in exchange for his freedom?

Answers:
1. Leoncico.
2. Made human sacrifices.
3. A roomful of gold.

▼ The Spanish and the Aztecs fought fierce battles, but the Spanish won in the end – mainly because they had guns, and the Aztecs didn't.

35 **To conquer the Inca people of Peru, Francisco Pizarro, another explorer, played a nasty trick.** In 1532, he captured Atahuallpa, the Inca leader. Atahuallpa said that if Pizarro set him free, he would give him a room filled to the ceiling with gold. Pizarro agreed. But once Atahuallpa had handed over the gold, Pizarro killed him anyway. Then he took over Cuzco, the Inca capital city. Cuzco was high in the mountains, and Pizarro didn't like it. So he started a new capital city at Lima. Today, Lima is the capital city of Peru.

Around the world

▶ Ferdinand Magellan was a clever man who was very good at maths and science. These skills helped him on his exploration.

▲ Magellan set off from Spain on his round-the-world trip. X marks the spot where Magellan died.

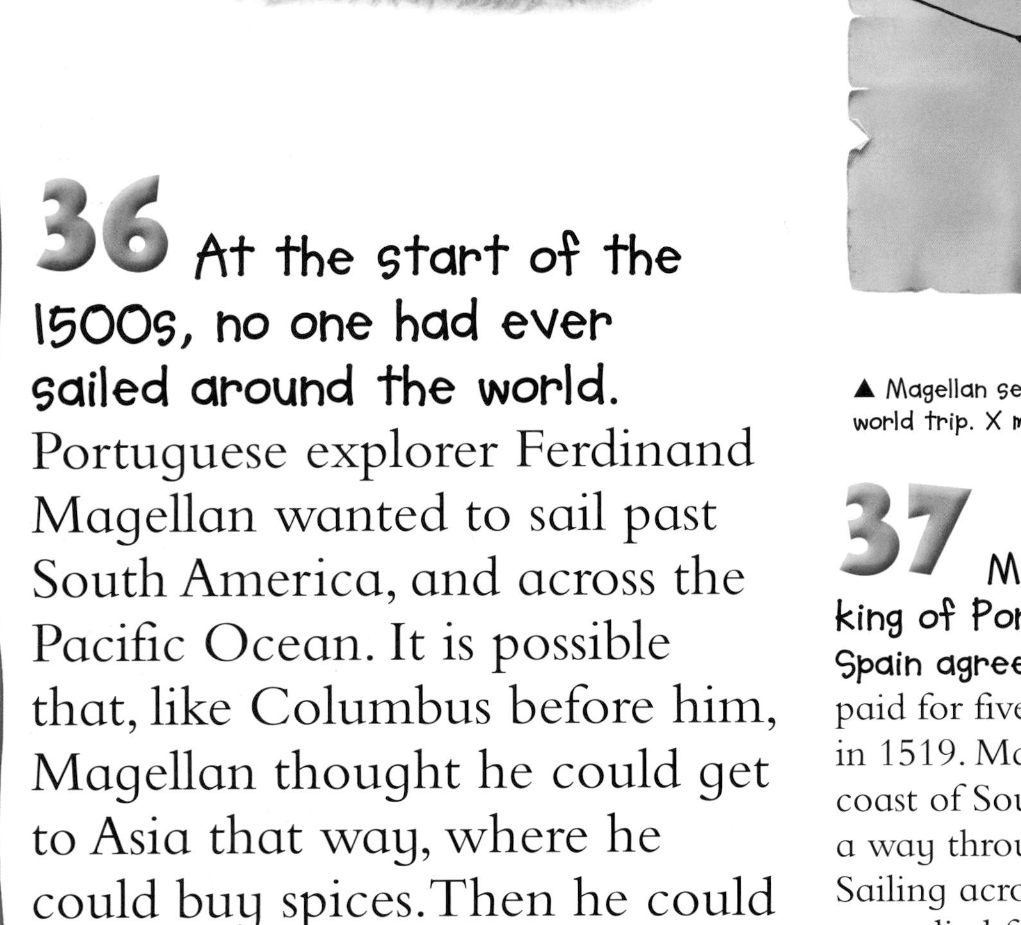

36 At the start of the 1500s, no one had ever sailed around the world. Portuguese explorer Ferdinand Magellan wanted to sail past South America, and across the Pacific Ocean. It is possible that, like Columbus before him, Magellan thought he could get to Asia that way, where he could buy spices. Then he could sail home past India and Africa – a round-the-world trip.

37 Magellan fell out with the king of Portugal, but the king of Spain agreed to help him. The king paid for five ships and Magellan set off in 1519. Magellan sailed down the coast of South America until he found a way through to the Pacific Ocean. Sailing across the Pacific, many of the crew died from a disease called scurvy. It was caused by not eating enough fresh fruit and vegetables.

Francis Drake bought six tonnes of cloves in the Spice Islands. In England this was worth 10 million pounds in today's money.

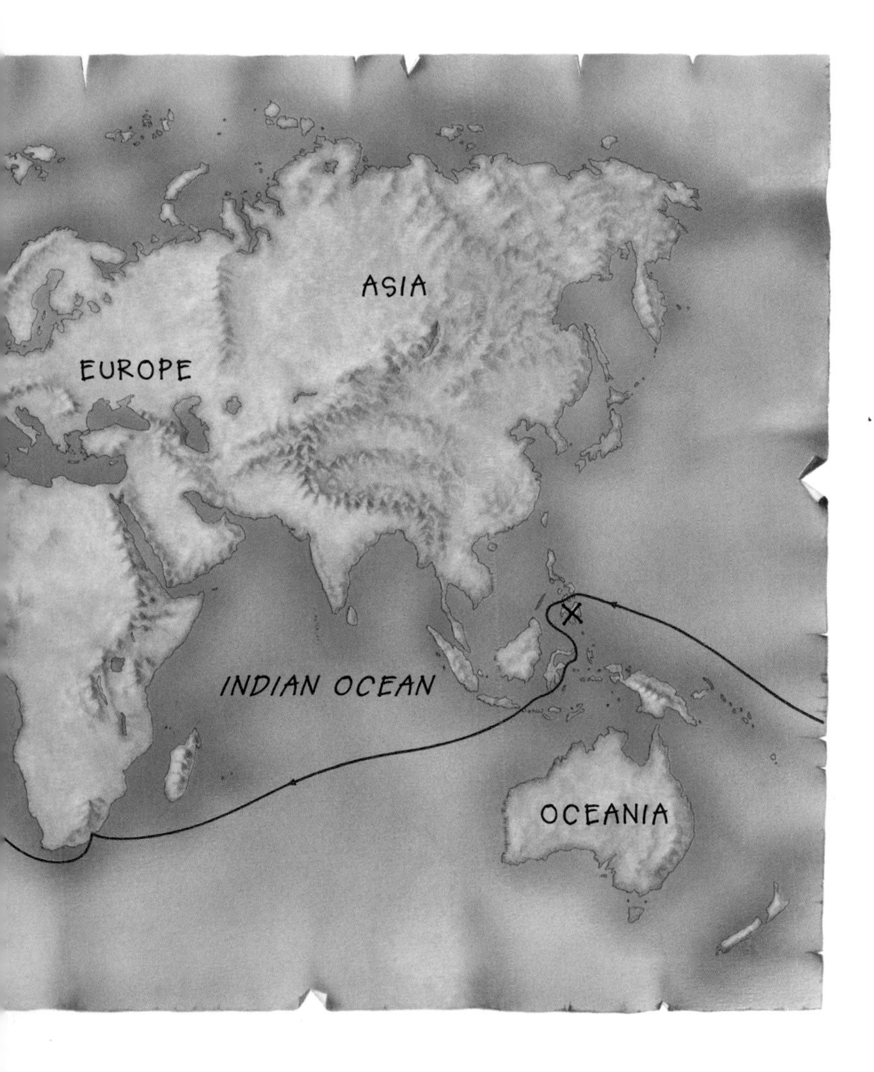

38 **Magellan made it across the Pacific – but then disaster struck.** After landing in the Philippines in 1521, Magellan made friends with the king of the island of Cebu. The king was fighting a war and he wanted Magellan to help him. Magellan and some of his crew went into battle, and Magellan was killed. The rest of the crew took two of the ships and escaped.

39 **In the end, just one of Magellan's ships made it back to Spain.** It picked up a cargo of spices in Indonesia and sailed home. Magellan had taken over 200 crew with him, but less than 20 of them returned. They were the first people to have sailed all the way around the world.

40 **Another 55 years went by before anyone sailed around the world again.** Queen Elizabeth I asked an English privateer (a kind of pirate) named Francis Drake to try a round-the-world trip in 1577. He made money on the way by robbing Spanish ships (the Queen said he could!). After his three-year voyage, Drake returned to England. Queen Elizabeth gave him a huge reward of £10,000.

EXPLORER QUIZ

Which of these foods would have helped to save Magellan's men from scurvy?

a. Lemon juice
b. Burger in a bun
c. Glass of milk
d. Cabbage
e. Chocolate cake

Answers:
a. and d.

Captain Cook

41 Captain James Cook spent just 11 years exploring, from 1768 to 1779. But he was still one of the greatest explorers. Cook sailed all over the Pacific Ocean and made maps that have helped sailors ever since. He also sailed around the world, north to the Arctic, and south to the Antarctic.

▼ As well as studying the planets, Cook took wildlife experts with him on his explorations. They collected plants that weren't known in Europe, and drew sketches and made notes about them.

Pen holder

Dividers

42 In 1768 the British navy asked Cook to go on an important mission. He was to go to the Pacific island of Tahiti, to make measurements and observations of the planet Venus passing in front of the Sun. After that, Cook went to look for a new continent in the far south – but he didn't find one. Instead, he explored Australia, New Zealand and the Pacific Islands and made new maps.

Parallel ruler

Sector

◀ Cook needed high-quality drawing instruments to help him make his measurements for maps.

43 Many people still believed there was an unknown continent in the south. So they sent Cook back to look for it again in 1772. He sailed further south than anyone had been before, until he found the sea was frozen solid. Cook sailed all the way around Antarctica, but he was never close enough to land to see it. It wasn't explored until 1820, nearly 50 years later.

James Cook was born into a very poor family and became a sailor after he ran away to sea to seek his fortune.

44 For Cook's third voyage, he headed north. He wanted to see if he could find a sea route between the Pacific Ocean and the Atlantic Ocean, across the top of Canada. After searching for it in 1778, he went to spend the winter in Hawaii. At first, the Hawaiians thought Cook was a god named Lono!

I DON'T BELIEVE IT!

Captain Cook was the first European to discover Hawaii, in 1778. He called it the Sandwich Islands.

45 Cook found his way around better than any sailor before him. An inventor named John Harrison had created a new clock (called the chronometer) that could measure the time precisely, even at sea. Before that, clocks had pendulums, so they didn't work on ships. From the time that the sun went down, Cook could work out exactly how far east or west he was.

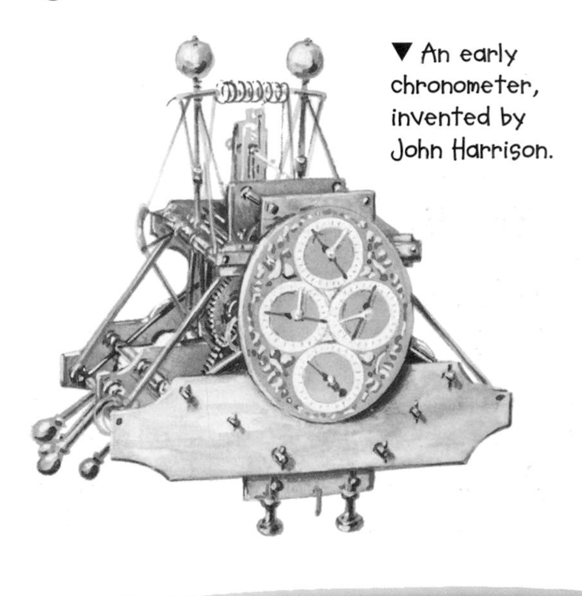

▼ An early chronometer, invented by John Harrison.

Crossing America

46 The United States of America was created in 1776 – less than 250 years ago. At that time, there were huge parts of it that still hadn't been explored. In 1803, the third president of the USA, Thomas Jefferson, asked Meriwether Lewis to go exploring. Lewis asked his friend William Clark to go with him.

▼ After the Missouri grew too narrow for their boat, Lewis and Clark's team used canoes. Local Native American guides helped them to paddle and find their way.

47 Lewis and Clark planned to travel all the way across America to the Pacific Ocean. They built a special boat for sailing on rivers. The boat could be rowed, pushed along with a pole, or towed with a rope. It also had sails for catching the wind. They took a crew of about 40 men, and in May 1804, they set off from the city of St Louis, sailing along the Missouri River.

48 In North Dakota, Lewis and Clark made a new friend – Sacagawea. She was a Shoshone Native American who joined the expedition as a guide. She helped Lewis and Clark to make friends with the Native American peoples they met during their trip. She knew where to find plants that they could eat and how to make tools. She also saved a pile of valuable papers that were about to fall into the river.

▶ It's thought that Sacagawea died a few years after the Lewis and Clark expedition, aged just 25 or 26.

Sacagawea took her newborn baby on the trip across America!

49 During the trip, Lewis and Clark were scared by bears. One day, Lewis was out hunting when a grizzly bear chased him. Lewis tried to shoot it, but he was out of bullets. The bear chased him into a river, but Lewis was in luck – the bear changed its mind and walked away.

MAKE A TOTEM POLE

You will need:

scissors cardboard tube paper felt-tip pens glue

1. Cut strips of paper long enough to wrap around the tube.
2. Draw faces, monsters and birds on the strips, then glue them around the tube.
3. Make wings from paper and glue them to the back of the tube.
4. Make a beak by cutting out a triangle, folding it in half and gluing it to the front of the tube.

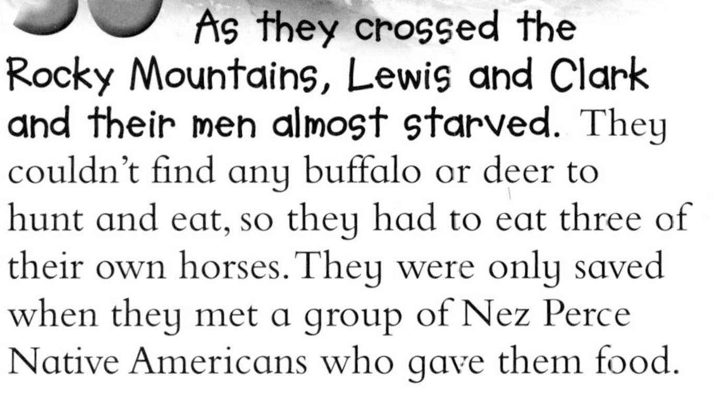

51 The crew paddled in canoes along the Columbia River to the sea. They reached the Pacific Ocean in November 1805 – then turned around and trekked all the way back. When they got home, Lewis and Clark were national heroes. The president gave them money and land.

50 As they crossed the Rocky Mountains, Lewis and Clark and their men almost starved. They couldn't find any buffalo or deer to hunt and eat, so they had to eat three of their own horses. They were only saved when they met a group of Nez Perce Native Americans who gave them food.

▶ Lewis and Clark were in danger of getting badly lost in the Rocky Mountains. The locals who showed them the way and gave them food saved their lives.

Exploring Africa

52 When Europeans began exploring Africa, they found it could be deadly.

In 1795, Scottish doctor Mungo Park went to explore the Niger River, in West Africa. Along the way, Park was robbed, kept prisoner, had all his clothes stolen, almost died of thirst and fell ill with a fever. However, he still went back to Africa in 1805.

Mungo Park

▶ Livingstone made many of his journeys by boat. On one occasion, his boat collided with a hippo and overturned, causing him to lose some of his equipment.

TRUE OR FALSE?

1. Victoria Falls is a giant cliff.
2. Timbuktu is in the Sahara Desert.
3. Henry Stanley found Dr Livingstone in New York.
4. David Livingstone was eaten by a lion.

Answers:
1 FALSE. It's a huge waterfall.
2. TRUE 3 FALSE. He found him in Tanzania, Africa.
4. FALSE A lion attacked him, but he escaped with an injured arm.

53 Dr David Livingstone was one of the most famous explorers of Africa.

He went there in 1840 as a missionary, to try to teach African people to be Christians. He trekked right across the dusty Kalahari Desert with his wife and young children and discovered Lake Ngami. He was also mauled by a lion, so badly that he could never use his left arm again.

When Dr Livingstone died, his heart was buried in Africa while the rest of his body was sent home to England.

54 Dr Livingstone kept exploring and became the first European to travel all the way across Africa. On the way, he discovered a huge, beautiful waterfall on the Zambezi River. The locals called it Mosi Oa Tunya, meaning 'the smoke that thunders'. Livingstone renamed it Victoria Falls, after Britain's Queen Victoria.

▲ At their centre, the Victoria Falls are 108 metres high.

55 In 1869, Dr Livingstone went missing. He had gone exploring in East Africa and no one had heard from him. Everyone thought he had died. An American writer, Henry Stanley, went to look for Livingstone. He found him in the town of Ujiji, in Tanzania. He greeted him with the words: "Dr Livingstone, I presume?"

▼ It took Henry Stanley eight months to find Dr Livingstone in Africa.

56 French explorer René Caillié went exploring in disguise. He wanted to see the ancient city of Timbuktu in the Sahara Desert, but only Muslims were allowed in. He dressed up as an Arab trader and sneaked into the city in 1828. He was the first European to go there and return home alive.

The source of the Nile

57 In the ancient world, the Nile was an important river. It provided the Egyptians with water, and the Greeks and Romans knew about it too. Ancient explorers tried to sail up the Nile to see where it went, but they kept getting stuck. An Egyptian named Ptolemy drew a map of the Nile, showing it flowing from a big lake in the middle of Africa.

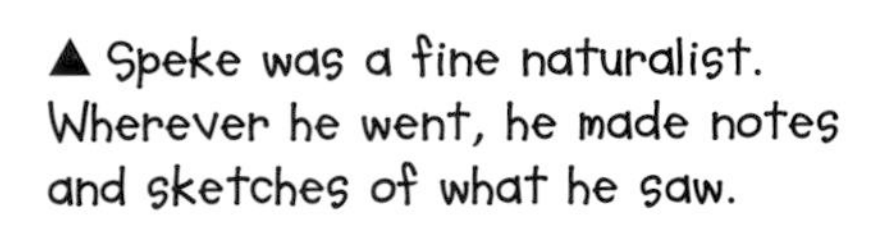

▲ Speke was a fine naturalist. Wherever he went, he made notes and sketches of what he saw.

▲ Richard Burton was an English army officer who learned to speak 29 languages.

58 In the 1800s, explorers still wanted to find the beginning, or 'source', of the Nile. In 1856, two British explorers named Richard Burton and John Speke set off to find it. They trekked across Africa to look for the big lake. Both men soon caught the disease malaria from mosquito bites. Burton became so ill he had to stop and rest.

▶ The Nile is the world's longest river. It flows across the entire length of the desert lands of Egypt.

Burton and Speke survived malaria, but it is the most deadly disease in the world. It has killed more people than all the wars in history put together.

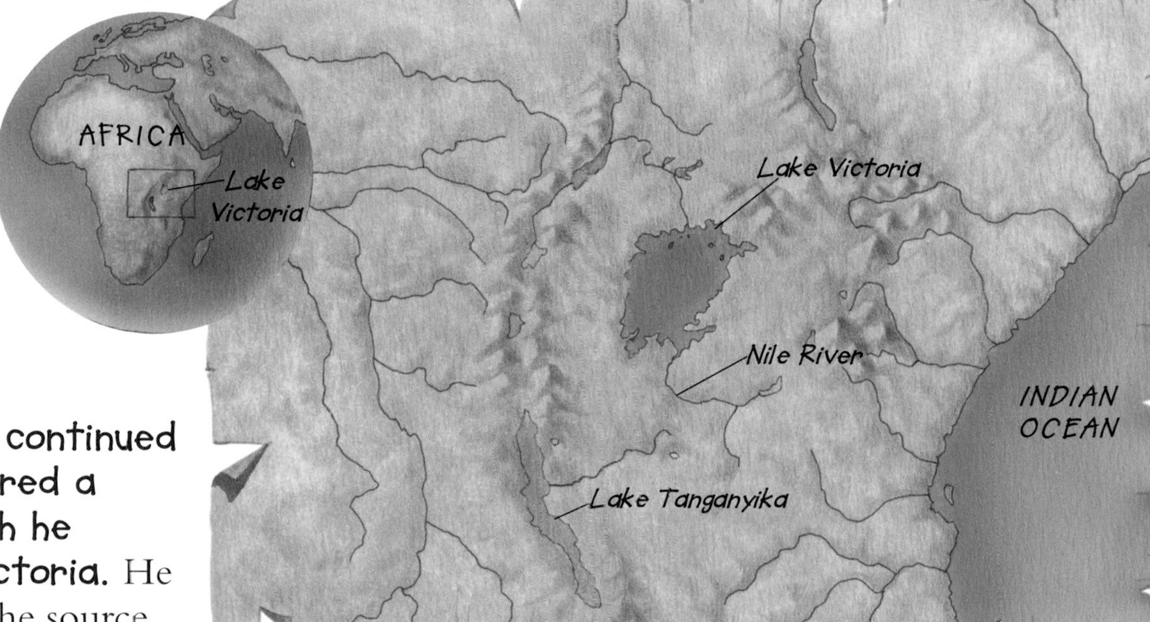

▶ As it turned out, Ptolemy was right. The Nile does flow from a great lake in the middle of Africa – Lake Victoria.

59 **Speke continued on and discovered a huge lake, which he named Lake Victoria.** He was sure it was the source of the Nile. He returned to Britain and told everyone he had found the source. Burton was furious. Speke went back to Africa to explore the lake, and found the place where the Nile flows out of it.

60 **Meanwhile, two other explorers were sailing up the Nile to find the source.** They were a married couple, Samuel and Florence White Baker. In 1864, they had sailed so far up the Nile that they met Speke coming the other way. The mystery of where the Nile began had been solved once and for all.

Exploring Australia

▶ The didgeridoo is a traditional musical instrument made from a hollowed out tree trunk. It is an important part of the historical culure of the aboriginal people.

61 People settled in Australia more than 50,000 years ago. The aboriginal people have lived there ever since. Just 400 years ago, in the early 1600s, sailors from Europe began to explore Australia. Britain claimed Australia for itself, and lots of British people went to live there.

62 European settlers were sure there was a huge sea in the middle of Australia. In 1844, a soldier named Charles Sturt went to look for the sea. He found that the middle of Australia was a hot, dry desert (now called the outback). His men got sunburn and scurvy, and their fingernails crumbled to dust. Sturt himself nearly went blind. But he had proved the mythical sea did not exist.

▼ Burke and Wills took over 40 horses and camels on their expedition. The camels were from India, as they were well suited to Australia's dry climate.

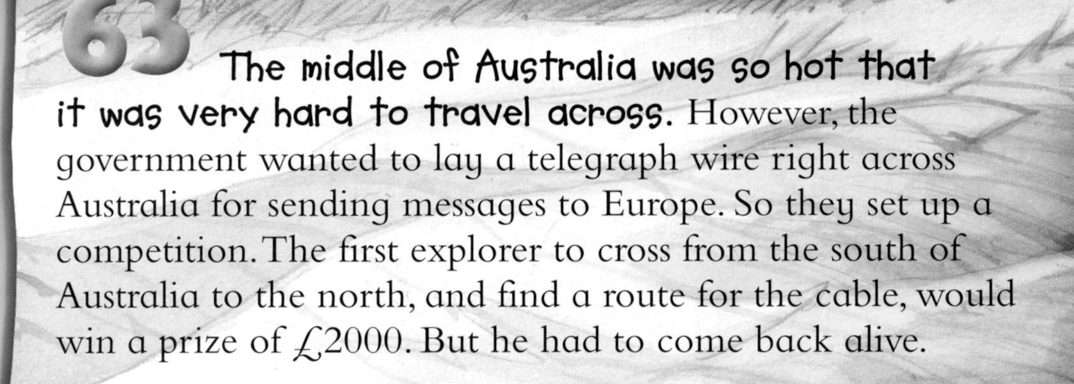

63 The middle of Australia was so hot that it was very hard to travel across. However, the government wanted to lay a telegraph wire right across Australia for sending messages to Europe. So they set up a competition. The first explorer to cross from the south of Australia to the north, and find a route for the cable, would win a prize of £2000. But he had to come back alive.

Camels were imported all the way from India for Burke and Wills' expedition!

64 Irishman Robert Burke decided to try for the prize.

He set off in 1860 with a team of horses and camels. Four men – Burke, William Wills, and two others – made it all the way across Australia. On the way back one man died, and they stopped to bury him. The rest of the team, waiting to meet them, gave up and went home. The three survivors were left alone in the desert, and Burke and Wills starved to death. Only one man lived – he was rescued by Aborigines.

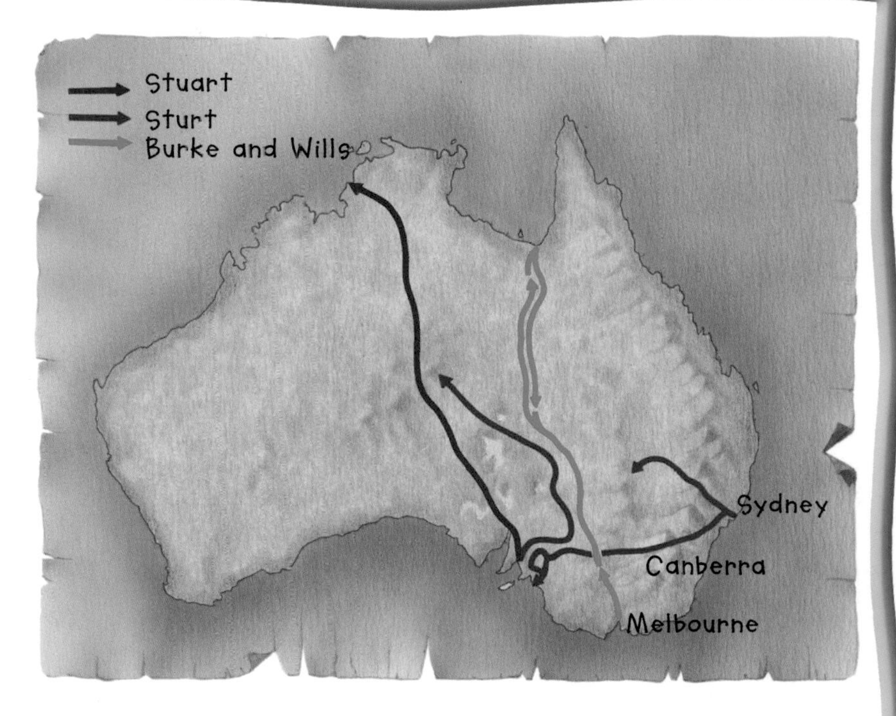

▲ Only Stuart's expedition was completely successful. His journey opened up the interior of Australia for settlement and farming.

65 Meanwhile, another explorer was racing Burke for the prize.

John McDouall Stuart took a different route across Australia, further west than Burke's. Unlike Burke, Stuart made it back alive – but he almost died. When he came home to Adelaide to claim his prize, he was so sick he had to be carried on a stretcher.

EXPLORER QUIZ

The Aborigines could survive in the outback because they knew what foods to eat and where to find them. Which of these foods could Burke's men have eaten?

1. Bunya nut.
2. Wichetty grub (a kind of baby insect).
3. Seaweed.
4. Ostrich eggs.
5. Wild honey.

Answers:
1, 2 and 5. Not ostrich eggs, as ostriches are only found in Africa. Not seaweed, as it is only found in the sea.

Arctic adventures

66 The Arctic is the land and sea around the North Pole. Explorers first went there to search for the Northwest Passage – the sea-route leading from the Atlantic Ocean to the Pacific Ocean. They spent 400 years trying to find it, and many explorers died of cold or drowned in the Arctic Ocean.

67 Norwegian explorer Roald Amundsen was the first to sail through the Northwest Passage. Amundsen used a small fishing boat that made it easier to sail along shallow channels and between chunks of floating ice. But the journey still took him three years – from 1903 to 1906. Amundsen learned a lot about surviving in the cold from local peoples he met on the way.

68 There was still part of the Arctic where no one had been – the North Pole. Another Norwegian explorer, Fridtjof Nansen, built a ship called the *Fram*, which was designed to get stuck in the ice without being damaged. As the ice moved, it carried the *Fram* nearer to the Pole. Nansen almost reached the Pole in 1895 – but not quite.

After Nansen had finished his journey to the North Pole in the *Fram*, Amundsen used the same ship to go to the South Pole.

69 Next, an American named Robert Peary and his assistant Matthew Henson, set off for the North Pole. Peary had always wanted to be the first to get there. After two failed attempts, Peary used dogsleds and Inuit guides to help him reach the pole in the year 1909.

▲ Peary and Henson used traditional sealskin clothes for their journey, and paid local Inuit people to make their clothes and equipment.

70 When Peary announced that he had been to the Pole, he was in for a shock. Another explorer, Frederick Cook, who had been Peary's friend, said he had got there first! The two men had an argument. Then it was revealed that Cook had lied about another expedition. After that, nobody believed he had been to the North Pole either.

◀ Fridtjof Nansen's boat, the *Fram*, was specially shaped so that when it was squeezed by ice, it lifted up instead of getting crushed. This allowed the ship to move safely with the ice towards the North Pole.

I DON'T BELIEVE IT!

Some experts think Peary didn't actually reach the North Pole. If this is true then the first person at the North Pole was Wally Herbert, who walked there in 1969.

Antarctic adventures

71 Antarctica was explored less than 200 years ago. This large and mountainous continent is at the southern tip of the Earth. It is even colder than the Arctic and very dangerous. In the early 1900s, explorers such as Robert Scott and Ernest Shackleton tried to reach the South Pole and failed. In 1909, Shackleton came within 155 kilometres of the South Pole, but had to turn back.

72 In 1910, British explorer Robert Scott decided to set off for the South Pole again. He took motor sleds and ponies to carry all his supplies. He decided that when his men got near the Pole, they would pull their own sleds. In Antarctica, he also wanted to collect rock samples to study.

73 Meanwhile, Roald Amundsen was on his way to try to reach the North Pole. But when he heard that Robert Peary had already got there, he decided to race Scott to the South Pole instead. Amundsen used different methods from Scott – sleds pulled by husky dogs carried supplies.

▶ Amundsen's team used lightweight dogsleds. If a dog died or became too weak to go on, it was fed to the other dogs. This reduced the amount of food the men had to carry.

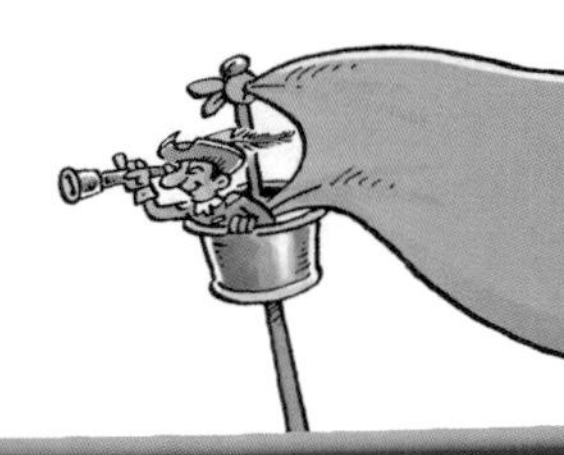

When Amundsen set off for the South Pole, he had already made several journeys to leave food stores at stages along the route.

▲ When Scott's team reached the South Pole, they took photos of each other, but their faces showed how upset they were not to be there first.

74 **In 1911, both Scott and Amundsen reached Antarctica, and set off for the South Pole.** Amundsen left first and got there quickly with his dogs. Scott's motor sleds broke down and his ponies died. His team trudged to the Pole, only to find Amundsen had been there first. On the way back, Scott's men got stuck in a blizzard. They ran out of food, and died of cold and hunger.

75 **Shackleton never got to the South Pole – but he had a very exciting Antarctic adventure.** He wanted to trek across Antarctica in 1914. But before he could start, his ship, the *Endurance*, was crushed by the ice. The crew were left on the frozen ocean with just three lifeboats. Shackleton left his men on an island while he took one tiny boat to get help. He had to cross a stormy ocean and climb over icy mountains before he found a village. All his men were rescued and came home safely.

Scientific searches

76 Lots of great explorers were scientists. Some went exploring to find rocks and minerals, or to study mountains or seas. Some were looking for new species (types) of plants and animals. Today, scientists explore in jungles, deserts and oceans to look for things no one else has found before.

▲ Darwin studied the many different types of finches on the Galapagos Islands.

77 Charles Darwin went on a round-the-world voyage on a ship called the *Beagle*, from 1831 to 1836. As the ship's naturalist (nature expert), it was Darwin's job to collect new species. He found all kinds of birds, plants, lizards, insects and other living things. He found many strange fossils too. Back in England, Darwin wrote lots of important books about the natural world.

▲ Darwin made notes about his findings. He believed that plants and animals changed to suit their surroundings.

▼ The horses we know today developed gradually from smaller horselike animals over a period of about 55 million years. Darwin called this process of gradual change evolution.

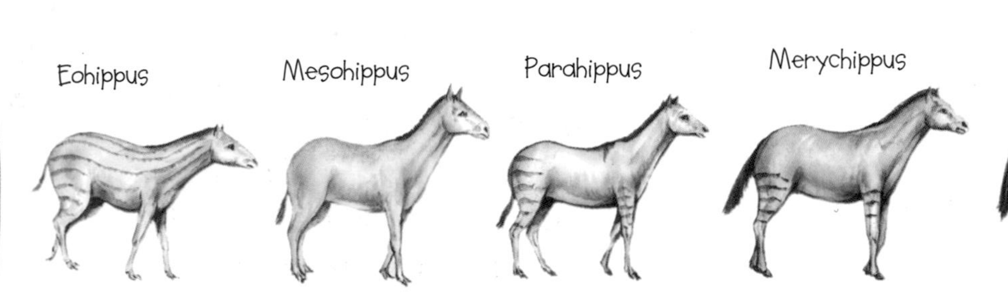

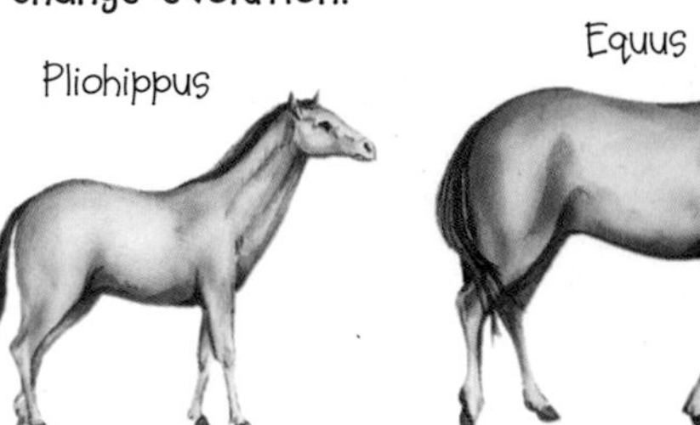

The sea current that flows up the west coast of South America was named in honour of Von Humboldt.

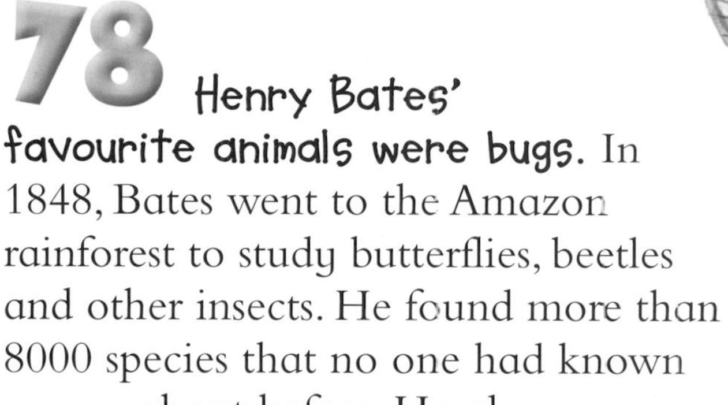

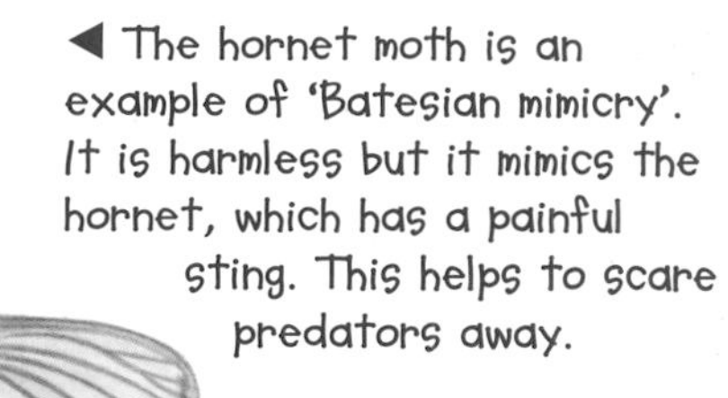

◀ The hornet moth is an example of 'Batesian mimicry'. It is harmless but it mimics the hornet, which has a painful sting. This helps to scare predators away.

Hornet moth

78 Henry Bates' favourite animals were bugs.

Henry Bates' favourite animals were bugs. In 1848, Bates went to the Amazon rainforest to study butterflies, beetles and other insects. He found more than 8000 species that no one had known about before. He also discovered that some harmless animals look like poisonous animals to stay safe. Today, this is called 'Batesian mimicry' (mimicry means copying).

Hornet

TRUE OR FALSE?

1. Henry Bates discovered more than 8000 species of insects.
2. Aimé Bonpland was an expert on local medicines.
3. Darwin's ship was called the *Basset*.
4. Mary Kingsley became caught in an animal trap.

Answers:
1.TRUE 2.FALSE Aimé Bonpland was a plant-expert.
3. FALSE Darwin's ship was called the *Beagle*.
4.TRUE

79

German scientist Alexander von Humboldt wanted to understand everything in the world. He and his friend, French plant-expert Aimé Bonpland, explored South America for five years between 1799 and 1804. They studied all kinds of things – poisonous plants, local medicines, ocean currents, rocks, rivers, mountains, and the stars at night. Later, Humboldt wrote a book, *Kosmos*, all about nature.

▶ Von Humboldt studied landscape extensively. The cold sea current that flows up the west coast of South America is named in his honour.

80

Mary Kingsley loved exploring rivers in Africa. She searched for new species – especially river fish – and studied the way of life of local rainforest people. On her travels, Kingsley fell into an animal trap full of spikes, got caught in a tornado, was cornered by an angry hippo and had a crocodile climb into her canoe.

Archaeological adventures

▲ The Nabataean people built many beautiful temples on the small plain at Petra.

81 Old ruined cities, palaces and tombs can stay hidden for centuries. Some get buried or covered with desert sand. Some are in faraway places where no one goes any more. When an explorer finds an ancient ruin, it can reveal lots of secrets about how people used to live long ago. Finding things out from ancient ruins is called archaeology.

82 Swiss explorer Johann Ludwig Burckhardt wanted to explore Africa. First he went to the Middle East to learn Arabic for his African trip. In 1812, in what is now Jordan, he discovered an amazing ruined city, carved out of red and yellow rock. It was Petra, the capital of the Nabataean people, built in the 2nd century. Burckhardt was the first European to go there.

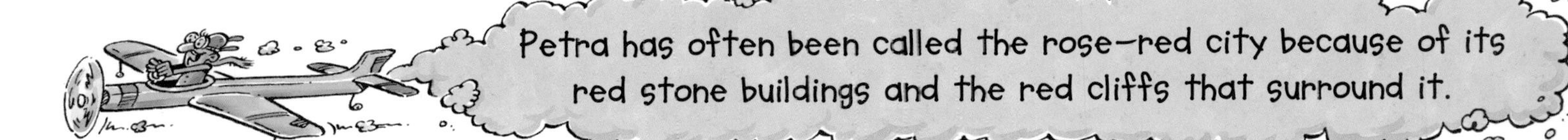

83 The city of Troy, which you can read about in the Greek myths, really existed. In 1870, German archaeologist Heinrich Schliemann travelled to Turkey to see if he could find Troy. He discovered the ruins of nine cities, one of which he thought was Troy. He found it had been destroyed and rebuilt many times. Schliemann also dug up piles of beautiful gold jewellery from the ruins.

◀ Schliemann's wife, Sophia, wearing some of the jewels found in the ruins uncovered by her husband.

84 In 1911, American explorer Hiram Bingham found a lost city, high on a mountain in Peru. The local people knew about it, and called it Machu Picchu, meaning 'old mountain', but the outside world had no idea it was there. Bingham wrote a book about his discovery, and today, half a million tourists visit it every year.

▲ The cave paintings at Lascaux depict animals such as bison, deer and horses.

MAKE A CAVE PAINTING

You will need:

paper (rough beige paper looks best)
red and black paint twigs

To make your painting look like real Lascaux cave art, use a twig dipped in paint to draw stick figures and animals such as cows, deer and cats. You can also try making patterns of spots using your fingertips.

85 Four teenagers exploring a cave stumbled upon some of the world's most important cave paintings. The cave was in Lascaux, France and the four boys found it in 1940, after a tree fell down, leaving a hole in the ground. Inside were passages leading to several rooms. The walls were covered with paintings of wild animals and humans who had lived 17,000 years ago.

The highest mountains

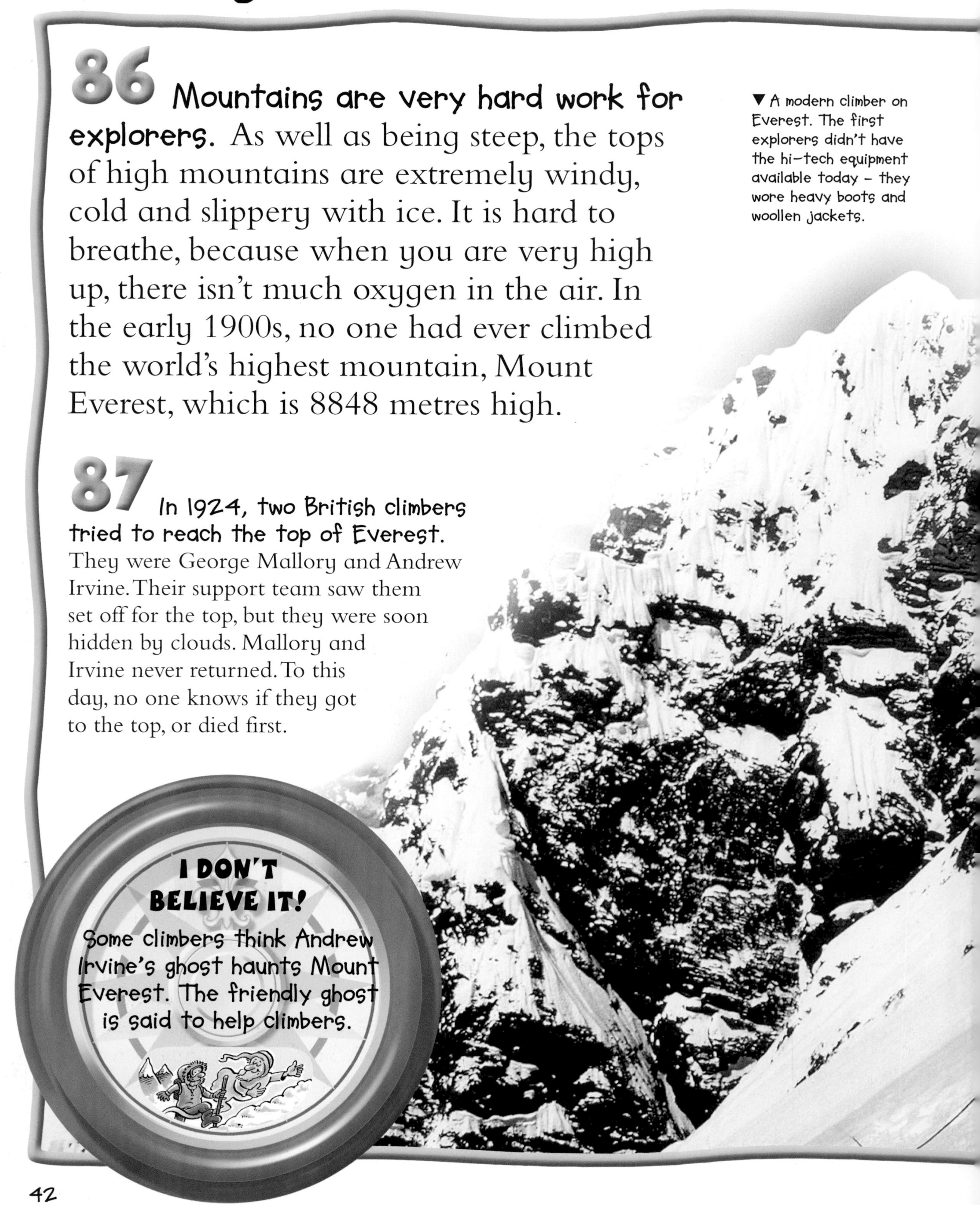

86 Mountains are very hard work for explorers. As well as being steep, the tops of high mountains are extremely windy, cold and slippery with ice. It is hard to breathe, because when you are very high up, there isn't much oxygen in the air. In the early 1900s, no one had ever climbed the world's highest mountain, Mount Everest, which is 8848 metres high.

▼ A modern climber on Everest. The first explorers didn't have the hi-tech equipment available today – they wore heavy boots and woollen jackets.

87 In 1924, two British climbers tried to reach the top of Everest. They were George Mallory and Andrew Irvine. Their support team saw them set off for the top, but they were soon hidden by clouds. Mallory and Irvine never returned. To this day, no one knows if they got to the top, or died first.

I DON'T BELIEVE IT!

Some climbers think Andrew Irvine's ghost haunts Mount Everest. The friendly ghost is said to help climbers.

88 In the 1950s, many countries were trying to send climbers to the top of Everest. A Swiss expedition nearly made it in 1952. In 1953, a British team set off. Two climbers, Evans and Bourdillon, climbed to within 90 metres of the summit, but had to turn back when an oxygen tank broke. Then, another two climbers tried. Their names were Edmund Hillary and Tenzing Norgay.

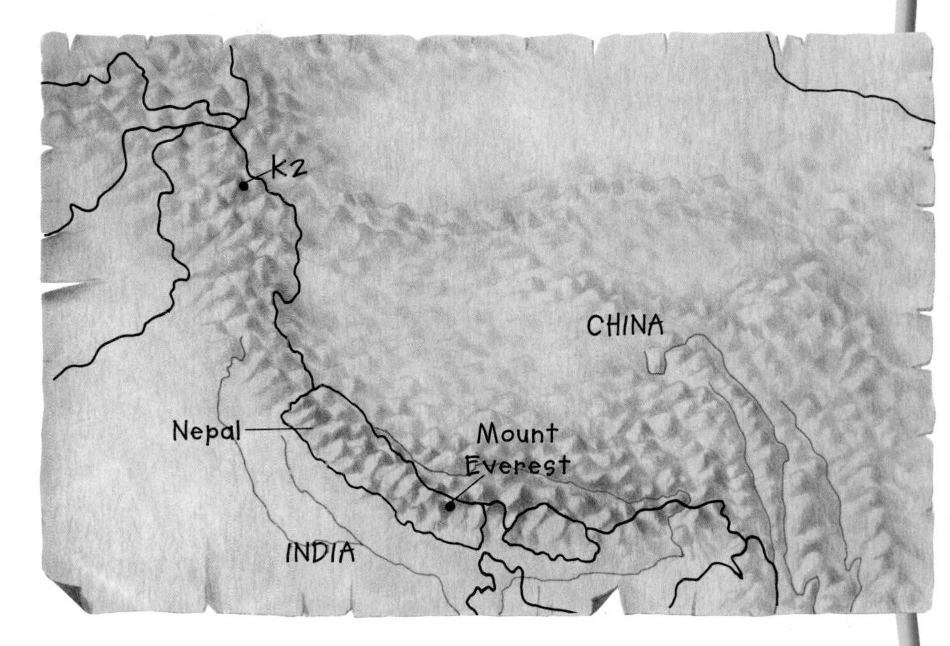

▲ Hillary and Norgay started their approach to Everest from its south side – which had been called unclimbable.

89 At 11.30 a.m. on 28 May, 1953, Tenzing and Hillary stood on top of Mount Everest. They hugged each other and took photos. They couldn't stay long, as they had to get back to their camp before their oxygen ran out. Hillary and Tenzing made it home safely, but many people have died trying to come back down Mount Everest after reaching the top.

90 There was still a mighty mountain yet to be climbed. K2, the world's second-highest mountain, is even more dangerous than Everest. People had been trying to climb it since 1902, and many had died. At last, in 1954, an Italian team succeeded. Lino Lacedelli and Achille Compagnoni were chosen to go to the top. Their oxygen ran out, but they kept going and reached the summit.

Under the sea

91 In 1872, a ship set out to explore a new world – the bottom of the sea. But the HMS *Challenger* wasn't a submarine. It measured the seabed, using ropes to find out the depth of the ocean. On its round-the-world voyage, *Challenger*'s crew also found many new species of sea creatures.

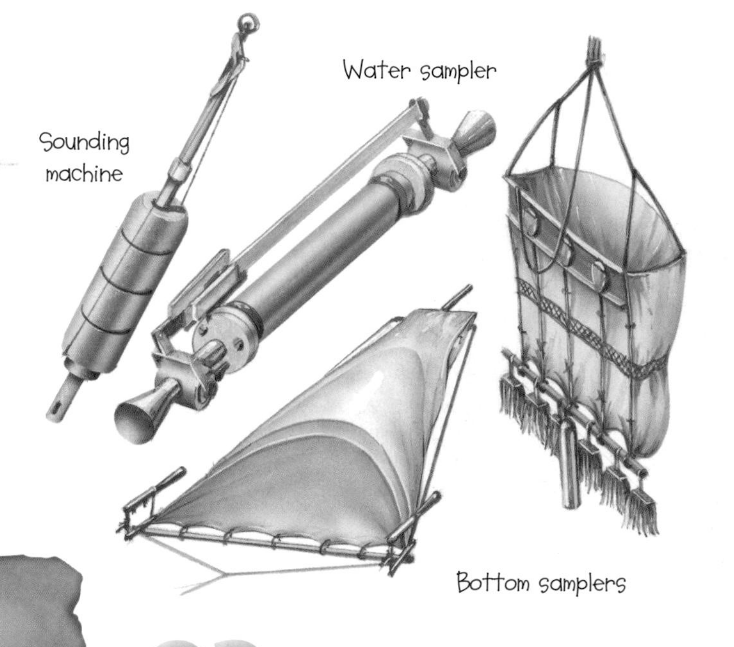

▲ HMS *Challenger* and some of the equipment her crew used to measure the shape and depth of the seabed all around the world.

TRUE OR FALSE?

1. The HMS *Challenger* was a submarine.
2. William Beebe was a wildlife specialist.
3. Beebe and Barton dived down into the Indian Ocean.
4. Scientists think that there are many new sea creatures that have not yet been discovered.

Answers:
1. FALSE It was a ship. 2. TRUE 3. FALSE Beebe and Barton dived down into the Atlantic Ocean. 4. TRUE

92 Lots of people still wanted to explore the seabed themselves. In 1928, an engineer, Otis Barton, and a wildlife professor, Wiliam Beebe, built the bathysphere, a round steel ball that could be lowered into the sea. In 1934, Beebe and Barton climbed inside and dived 923 metres down into the Atlantic Ocean.

Auguste Piccard was a balloon inventor before he designed *Trieste*.

93 Another inventor, Auguste Piccard, invented a craft called the bathyscaphe. It wasn't lowered from a ship, but could travel about by itself. In 1960, a bathyscaphe named *Trieste* took two passengers to the deepest part of the sea, Challenger Deep, in the Pacific Ocean. It is over 10,900 metres deep.

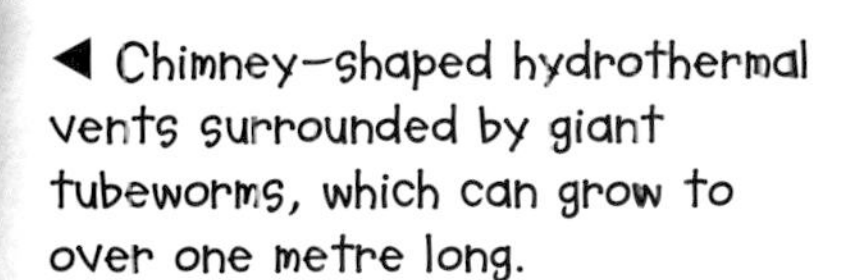

◀ Chimney-shaped hydrothermal vents surrounded by giant tubeworms, which can grow to over one metre long.

▲ The *Trieste*'s two passengers crouched inside the round part that you can see hanging below the main section.

94 In 1977, scientists discovered strange chimneys on the seabed and named them hydrothermal vents. Hot water from inside the Earth flowed out of these vents. The hot water contained minerals that living things could feed on. All around the vents were weird sea creatures that no one had ever seen before, such as giant tubeworms and giant clams.

95 The seas and oceans are so big, that parts of the undersea world are still unknown. There could be all kinds of strange sea caves and underwater objects we haven't found. Scientists think there could also be many new sea creatures, such as giant squid, sharks and whales, still waiting to be discovered.

Into space

96 There's still one place humans have hardly explored at all, and that's space. Space exploration started in October 1957, when *Sputnik I*, a Russian spacecraft, was launched. A rocket sent *Sputnik* into orbit around the Earth. But this first spacecraft had no passengers.

▼ Laika the space dog was a half-husky mongrel.

97 The first-ever astronaut went into space the same year. She wasn't a human, but a dog named Laika. She went into space aboard another Russian spacecraft, *Sputnik II*, in November 1957. Sadly, Laika died during the voyage, but she led the way for human space exploration.

▼ Yuri Gagarin in his space suit, shortly before leaving the planet to become the first ever human in space.

98 In 1961, Yuri Gagarin became the first human to go into space. His spacecraft was called *Vostok I*. After going into orbit, Gagarin flew once around the Earth, which took nearly two hours. Then *Vostok I* came back down to Earth, and landed safely. Gagarin's trip proved people could travel in space.

Yuri Gagarin travelled in *Vostok 1*, which circled the Earth at a speed of 27,400 kilometres an hour.

99

For hundreds of years, people dreamed of going to the Moon. Humans finally went there in 1969, aboard a US spacecraft called *Apollo 11*. The first person to stand on the Moon's surface was American astronaut Neil Armstrong, followed by Buzz Aldrin. They explored on the Moon for two hours and collected rocks. Then they flew safely back to Earth.

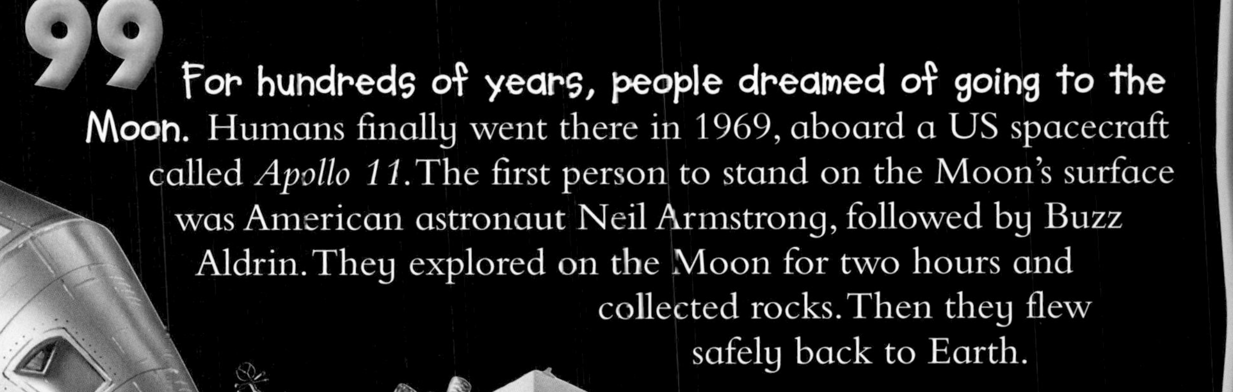

◀ The main capsule and Moon landing unit of the Apollo 11 spacecraft.

100

So far, no human has ever visited another planet. But we have sent space probes, with no one on board, millions of kilometres to explore the planets and other parts of space. The space probe *Voyager I*, launched in 1977, is still travelling. It is now more than ten billion kilometres away – the furthest humans have ever explored.

▲ The *Voyager I* unmanned space probe.

I DON'T BELIEVE IT!

Since Laika's journey in 1957, monkeys, a cat, frogs and spiders have all gone into space.

Index